MISSING!

THE WORLD'S GREATEST ART CRIMES

By ACE LANDERS

SCHOLASTIC INC.

No part of this publication may be reproduced, stored in a retrieval system, or transmitted in any form or by any means, electronic, mechanical, photocopying, recording, or otherwise, without written permission of the publisher. For information regarding permission, write to Scholastic Inc., Attention: Permissions Department, 557 Broadway, New York, NY 10012.

ISBN 978-0-545-64892-9

© 2014 Scholastic Inc. All rights reserved. Published by Scholastic Inc. SCHOLASTIC and associated logos are trademarks and/or registered trademarks of Scholastic Inc.

12 11 10 9 8 7 6 5 4 3 2   14 15 16 17 18/0

Printed in the U.S.A. 40
First printing, March 2014
Book design by Nancy Sabato
Photo research by Amla Sanghvi

Photo credits: Photographs ©: cover and box top (frame): AppStock/Shutterstock, Inc.; cover and box top inset: Andrew Howe/Getty Images; back cover (frame): AppStock/Shutterstock, Inc.; box cover product shot: © Scholastic Inc.; 1 and throughout (canvas background): Polina Katritch/Shutterstock, Inc.; 1 and throughout (frame): Iakov Filimonov/Shutterstock, Inc.; 4 top right: Modigliani, Amedeo/Musee d'Art Moderne de la Ville de Paris, Paris, France/Giraudon/The Bridgeman Art Library; 4 left: Braque, Georges/Private Collection, Paris, France/Peter Willi/The Bridgeman Art Library/© 2014 Artists Rights Society (ARS), New York/ADAGP, Paris; 4 bottom right: Leger, Fernand/Musee d'Art Moderne de la Ville de Paris, Paris, France/Giraudon/The Bridgeman Art Library/© 2014 Artists Rights Society (ARS), New York/ADAGP, Paris; 5 left: Picasso, Pablo/Musee d'Art Moderne de la Ville de Paris, Paris, France/Giraudon/The Bridgeman Art Library/© 2014 Estate of Pablo Picasso/Artists Rights Society (ARS), New York; 5 right & throughout (clipboard): Paket/Shutterstock, Inc.; 6: Vinci, Leonardo da/Louvre, Paris, France/Giraudon/The Bridgeman Art Library; 8: Eyck, Hubert & Jan van (after)/St. Bavo Cathedral, Ghent, Belgium/ Lukas - Art in Flanders VZW/Hugo Maertens/The Bridgeman Art Library; 9: Eyck, Hubert & Jan van/St. Bavo Cathedral, Ghent, Belgium/© Lukas - Art in Flanders VZW/Hugo Maertens/The Bridgeman Art Library; 10: Rembrandt Harmenszoon van Rijn/© Dulwich Picture Gallery, London, UK/The Bridgeman Art Library; 11: VisitBritain/Britain on View/Getty Images; 12 top: Medici/Mary Evans/The Image Works; 12 bottom: Degas, Edgar/Private Collection, Zurich, Switzerland/The Bridgeman Art Library; 13 top: Gogh, Vincent van/Buhrle Collection, Zurich, Switzerland/The Bridgeman Art Library; 13 bottom: Cezanne, Paul/Buhrle Collection, Zurich, Switzerland/The Bridgeman Art Library; 14: Rembrandt Harmenszoon van Rijn/© Nationalmuseum, Stockholm, Sweden/The Bridgeman Art Library; 15 top: Renoir, Pierre Auguste/© Nationalmuseum, Stockholm, Sweden/The Bridgeman Art Library; 15 bottom: Renoir, Pierre Auguste/© Nationalmuseum, Stockholm, Sweden/The Bridgeman Art Library; 16: Munch, Edvard/Nasjonalgalleriet, Oslo, Norway/The Bridgeman Art Library/© 2014 The Munch Museum/The Munch-Ellingsen Group/Artists Rights Society (ARS), New York; 17: Heiko Junge/SCANPIX/AP Images; 18: Rembrandt Harmenszoon van Rijn/© Isabella Stewart Gardner Museum, Boston, MA, USA/The Bridgeman Art Library; 20: Isabella Stewart Gardner Museum, Boston, MA, USA/The Bridgeman Art Library; 21 top: Flinck, Govaert/© Isabella Stewart Gardner Museum, Boston, MA, USA /The Bridgeman Art Library; 21 bottom: Manet, Edouard/© Isabella Stewart Gardner Museum, Boston, MA, USA/The Bridgeman Art Library; 22: Gogh, Vincent van/Van Gogh Museum, Amsterdam, The Netherlands/De Agostini Picture Library/The Bridgeman Art Library; 23 top: PAINTING/Alamy; 23 bottom: The Protected Art Archive/Alamy Images; 24: VoodooDot/Shutterstock, Inc.; 25 top: pongam/Shutterstock, Inc.; 25 center: stevanovicigor/Canstock; 25 bottom: Les and Dave Jacobs/Getty Images; 26 top: Matthew Cavanaugh/EPA/Newscom; 26 bottom: Egon Bömsch/imagebroker/Alamy Images; 27 top: Anthony Devlin/PA Wire/AP Images; 27 bottom: Laurent Cipriani/AP Images; 31: Francois Mori/dapd/AP Images; 32 center left: Vermeer, Jan (Johannes)/© Isabella Stewart Gardner Museum, Boston, MA, USA/The Bridgeman Art Library; 32 top: Rembrandt Harmenszoon van Rijn/© Isabella Stewart Gardner Museum, Boston, MA, USA/The Bridgeman Art Library; 32 bottom: Degas, Edgar/Private Collection/Photo © Christie's Images/The Bridgeman Art Library; 32 center right: Monet, Claude/Private Collection/Photo © Christie's Images/The Bridgeman Art Library.

TABLE OF CONTENTS

The Broken Security System: The Paris Museum of Modern Art Heist	5
Missing *Mona Lisa*	6
Salt Mines and Dynamite: The *Ghent Altarpiece* Heist	8
The Takeaway Rembrandt	10
Big Bührle Heist	12
BOOM! The Swedish National Museum Heist	14
"AHHHH!" Screamed *The Scream*	16
"Oh No!" Screamed *The Scream*, "Not Again!"	17
The Largest Museum Heist in History: Isabella Stewart Gardner Museum	18
The Shortest-Lived Art Heist: The Van Gogh Museum	22
The Van Gogh Museum: Take Two!	23
Priceless Protection	24
Who Finds Stolen Art?	26
The Art Loss Register	28
Crime Doesn't Pay ... But Art Crime Really Doesn't Pay!	30

STEALING IS BAD, BUT STEALING ART IS WORSE

In stealing art, a thief is not merely taking a replaceable object. A work by Picasso, Rembrandt, or Van Gogh is not a wallet or a cell phone. The crimes you are about to discover involve irreplaceable artifacts with massive cultural significance.

As you read on, consider how you would feel if your favorite books, your favorite films, or your favorite songs were suddenly taken from you, never to be experienced again. This is the sad fate of many stolen paintings — the world will never see them again. So please remember, while art theft might be interesting to read about, stealing a masterpiece is like stealing history itself.

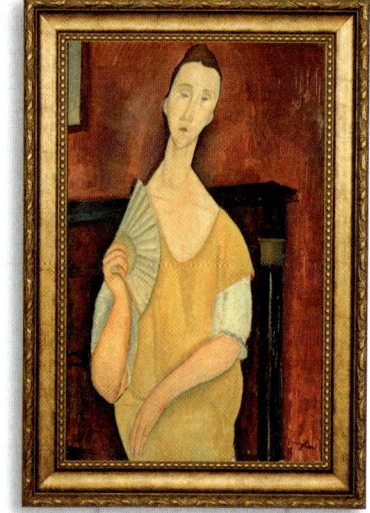
Woman with a Fan

Olive Tree Near Estaque

Still Life with Candle

THE BROKEN SECURITY SYSTEM:
THE PARIS MUSEUM OF MODERN ART HEIST

The Pigeon with Green Peas

DATE: May 19, 2010
LOCATION: Paris, France
MUSEUM: Museum of Modern Art
PAINTINGS: The Pigeon with Green Peas by Pablo Picasso
Pastoral by Henri Matisse
Olive Tree Near Estaque by Georges Braque
Woman with a Fan by Amedeo Modigliani
Still Life with Candle by Fernand Leger
THIEVES: AT LARGE!

In the middle of the night of May 19, 2010, a lone thief slipped into the Paris Museum of Modern Art completely undetected and made off with over one hundred million dollars' worth of paintings. Entering through a rear window, which he smashed open, the thief should have set off the museum's alarm system instantly, but as it turns out, the alarm system had been on the fritz for quite some time.

Even under the protection of security guards and a closed-circuit TV feed, the museum was still looted of five priceless paintings from artists including Picasso and Matisse. The thief moved swiftly and silently, removing each painting from its frame and exiting without raising any suspicion. The whole robbery took fifteen minutes. It wasn't until 7:00 a.m. that the security guards noticed that anything was wrong.

Since this heist, the paintings and the culprit are still at large.

MISSING MONA LISA

DATE: August 21, 1911
LOCATION: Paris, France
MUSEUM: Louvre
PAINTING: Mona Lisa by Leonardo da Vinci
THIEVES: CAPTURED!

Believe it or not, Leonardo da Vinci's famous painting, the *Mona Lisa*, was not always famous. Sure, it was a masterpiece with tremendous historical value to people in the art world, but Mona's secretive smile just wasn't as well-known as it is now. So what happened to raise her profile? It all came down to one fateful night in 1911.

Near closing time at the Louvre museum in Paris, three men hid themselves in a supply closet and stayed there overnight. During those precious hours, the men set their sights on one painting only: the *Mona Lisa*. The thieves worked their way through a massive protective glass case to finally get to the painting and its ornate frame. Then, in the morning, the three men stripped the painting from its frame, slipped out a back exit, and made off with the wooden canvas stashed under one of their coats.

The next morning, a visitor to the museum noticed that there was a blank wall with four iron hooks hanging where the *Mona Lisa* had once been. The Louvre security was immediately contacted, but they believed the painting was with a special set of photographers hired to catalog the museum's art. When the truth was revealed that the photographers did not have the painting, the museum was shut down for a week to investigate the crime.

After the museum reopened, droves of people flocked to see the "Mark of Shame" where the missing masterpiece should have been. Among the potential suspects were millionaires, politicians, and even other artists. The police even questioned Pablo Picasso! Newspaper headlines echoed the story around the world and just like that, the *Mona Lisa* became a household name.

Two years passed with no sign of the painting. Rumors of a reward for the *Mona Lisa* floated out and suddenly there was a new breakthrough in the case. In the end, the mastermind behind the theft turned out to be Vincenzo Perugia, an Italian native and employee of the Louvre! Not only was he an employee, but he was the very same worker who had installed the protective glass case around the *Mona Lisa*!

Perugia was caught trying to sell the painting to an art dealer in Florence, Italy. He claimed that his intentions were to return the *Mona Lisa* to Italy where it rightfully belonged. (Never mind that Leonardo da Vinci himself gave the painting to Francois I, the king of France.)

Perugia was brought before an Italian court in 1914, three years after his crime. The thief, who many in Italy considered a patriot, was given the minimum sentence. He only spent eight months in prison.

Now the *Mona Lisa* is back in her rightful home, hanging in the Louvre behind a climate-controlled, bulletproof glass case. For with great fame comes great risk. Over the years the painting has been vandalized by acid, rocks, spray paint, and even a teacup, but Leonardo's *Mona Lisa* smile is still winning over fans today and for years to come. About six million people visit her each year.

SALT MINES AND DYNAMITE:
THE *GHENT ALTARPIECE* HEIST

DATE: April 10, 1934
LOCATION: Ghent, Belgium
MUSEUM: Saint Bavo Cathedral
PAINTING: Ghent Altarpiece by Jan van Eyck
THIEVES: AT LARGE!

A masterpiece with a classically troubled life, the *Ghent Altarpiece*, also known as the *Adoration of the Mystic Lamb*, was painted in the fifteenth century by Jan van Eyck and his brother Hubert. Consisting of twelve panels, the full piece is 11-1/2 feet long and 15 feet high with hinges that allow the piece to be opened and closed to reveal two different scenes. It stands as the first truly successful oil painting in the world and also started a movement toward realistic art in Europe, which helped spark the Renaissance. In short, the *Ghent Altarpiece* is a marvelous wonder that has long been a target of art thieves and art aficionados under many guises.

Originally painted for a cathedral in Ghent, Belgium, the *Altarpiece* quickly gained notoriety. Over the next few centuries the painting would become a prize for invading armies. Napoleon stole the painting, but it was eventually returned to Ghent. Then parts of the painting were stolen and sold, ending up in a German museum. With the panels divided up and with World War I on the horizon, the precious painting was taken apart and hidden for its own safety, to finally be reunited only after the war was over.

This panel is called the *Just Judges*.

However, in 1934, thieves struck again, sneaking into the cathedral one night to steal the lower left panel known as the *Just Judges*. The theft was never solved and the panel is still missing to this day. In its place sits a replica painted by a copy artist. Believe it or not, though, this wasn't the final time a piece of the *Ghent Altarpiece* was stolen, and it was this final theft that seems the most outlandish.

During World War II, Hitler and the Nazis stole the painting, believing it to be an actual map that would lead them to religious relics. It did not lead them to any such artifacts, but it did come dangerously close to being destroyed. First by the falling bombs of wartime, and then when the Nazis moved the painting deep beneath the earth in an Austrian salt mine, along with other stolen pieces of art. As an insurance plan to keep the art from ever falling into the Allies' hands, the mine was rigged with dynamite, and set to explode and destroy every piece of valuable cultural artwork. Luckily, thanks to several miners, this never came to be, as these brave souls went against their leader's wishes and disarmed the dynamite to save these irreplaceable masterpieces.

THE TAKEAWAY REMBRANDT

While the *Ghent Altarpiece* has been stolen multiple times, only one, singular piece of artwork holds the dubious honor of having been the most stolen painting in the world in modern times: *The Portrait of Jacob de Gheyn III* by Rembrandt. Known as the Takeaway Rembrandt, it has been stolen four times since 1966, each time from the same art gallery.

The Dulwich Picture Gallery could never have known that this particular painting would become such a hot commodity. Sure, it's a Rembrandt, but it's hardly one of his most classic portraits. However, it is small, and at 12 by 10 inches, the painting is the perfect size for a quick getaway.

The first theft took place on New Year's Eve in 1966. A team of thieves drilled out an opening in one of the gallery's side doors and made off with eight paintings including the Takeaway Rembrandt. All the paintings were found a few days later when Scotland Yard was tipped off by an anonymous caller.

DATE: December 31, 1966, 1973, 1981, 1983
LOCATION: London, England
MUSEUM: Dulwich Picture Gallery
PAINTING: *The Portrait of Jacob de Gheyn III* by Rembrandt
THIEVES: AT LARGE!

Seven years later, the Takeaway Rembrandt was heisted for a second time in broad daylight by a visitor who simply lifted the painting off the wall, placed it in a plastic bag, and walked right out of the front door with it. He was arrested minutes after he left the museum, but when asked why he had stolen the painting, the thief said only that the piece struck him so much that he wanted to sketch it — so he took it. The painting was returned and put back on display immediately.

The Takeaway Rembrandt was stolen for a third time in 1981, by thieves posing as visitors to the gallery. As one thief distracted the security guard on duty, the other lifted the painting directly off the wall. Once again it was the only painting targeted, and once again it was recovered. This time the painting was found two weeks later in the trunk of a taxicab.

Finally, after three thefts, the Dulwich Gallery upgraded their security system. They even bolted the Takeaway Rembrandt to the wall. But this all proved useless, as the painting was stolen for a fourth time in 1983. These thieves entered from the skylight in the ceiling. They used a crowbar to yank the bolted painting from the wall, which set off the new alarm system, but the criminals disappeared before the police showed up three minutes later.

This time the Takeaway Rembrandt went missing for three years, but in 1986, after yet another anonymous tip, the

Inside the Dulwich Picture Gallery.

painting was found in West Germany, wrapped in paper and placed in three protective boxes sitting in a railway station. No arrests were ever made. The painting can still be seen at the Dulwich Picture Gallery in the Rembrandt Room . . . hopefully.

BIG BÜHRLE HEIST

Poppies Near Vétheuil

Count Lepic and His Daughters

DATE: February 10, 2008
LOCATION: Zurich, Switzerland
MUSEUM: E.G. Bührle Foundation Collection
PAINTINGS: Poppies Near Vétheuil by Claude Monet
Count Lepic and His Daughters by Edgar Degas
Blossoming Chestnut Branches by Vincent Van Gogh
The Boy in the Red Vest by Paul Cézanne
THIEVES: **CAPTURED!**

The Bührle Collection is one of the top private museums for Impressionist and Post-Impressionist art in Europe. However, to most people it is relatively unknown. On February 10, 2008, three masked men made their mark and ushered the museum onto the global stage of intrigue.

Shortly before closing time, three men in ski masks rushed into the museum. One of the thieves pulled a handgun and commanded everyone to lie down on the floor. As the patrons huddled close to the ground, the other thieves tore the paintings down from the wall and they escaped.

At the time this was the biggest art theft in European history with a value of over $160 million dollars ... and that was for only four paintings, all of which were displayed in one room of the Bührle Collection. The thieves raced off in a white van with the paintings still sticking out the back window.

Blossoming Chestnut Branches

What made the crime even more shocking was that it was the second massive art theft in Switzerland in less than a week! Prior to this crime, a separate set of thieves had stolen a pair of Picassos worth an estimated four and a half million dollars from another Swiss museum.

However, famous art pieces of this caliber are not easy to sell, even in underground criminal circles. The Monet and the Van Gogh were found a week after the heist, stashed in an abandoned car in Zurich, but the Degas and Cézanne had vanished with the criminals. The only trace the thieves had left behind was an accent.

During the robbery, the hostages had listened very closely to the thieves' orders . . . so closely that when interviewed by police, the hostages noted that one of the thieves spoke German with a Serbian accent. It was a small piece of information, but it paid off big-time.

A year later the Degas painting was returned to a Swiss museum after a large reward was offered, but the Cézanne's whereabouts remained a mystery. Knowing that there could possibly be a Serbian connection, the Swiss police looped the Serbian police into the investigation. Four years later, in 2012, the Cézanne was finally discovered in Belgrade, hidden in a suspect's car between the upholstered ceiling interior and the car frame. The thieves had finally tried to sell the masterpiece for a mere four and a half million dollars . . . though the painting was worth one hundred and ten million dollars. The painting was recovered all thanks to the sharp ears of a few museum patrons who were in the wrong place at the wrong time.

The Boy in the Red Vest

BOOM! THE SWEDISH NATIONAL MUSEUM HEIST

Rembrandt self-portrait

DATE: December 22, 2000
LOCATION: Stockholm, Sweden
MUSEUM: Swedish National Museum
PAINTINGS: A self-portrait by Rembrandt
Conversation by Pierre-Auguste Renoir
A Young Parisienne by Pierre-Auguste Renoir
THIEVES: **CAPTURED!**

If ever there was an art heist that played out in real life like an action movie, it happened at the Swedish National Museum. One crisp morning in December, the streets of Stockholm were bustling with people going to work or racing to finish their holiday shopping. It was a lovely day. Then the explosions started.

Loud booms ripped through the early morning as several car bombs were detonated at different areas around the city. No one knew what was going on. The police acted immediately, sending help in every direction. At first the attacks were attributed to terrorists, but there was more to this surprise than met the eye.

With the police embroiled in damage control, the Swedish National Museum was ripe for a heist. The car bombs had been an elaborate smokescreen to tie up the police and keep them busy while the real crime was happening across town.

A lone car drove down the only street leading to or from the museum. The Swedish National Museum is located on a peninsula

Conversation

and looks out over a river that runs through the city. The car parked directly in front of the museum and three people in ski masks got out. Armed with machine guns, they rushed inside.

The museum was crowded with visitors, but the thieves shouted at them to stay down. Over the next forty minutes, the men roamed through hallways filled with masterpieces and selected three paintings. When the police discovered that the museum was being robbed, they tried their best to get there but the roads were filled with diverted traffic from the blasts. The police were trapped outside of the crime zone.

This seemingly meant that the criminals were trapped *inside* the crime zone. However, this was all according to plan. Instead of exiting through the front door and returning to their car, the thieves made their getaway on a speedboat waiting for them on the river behind the museum. In just under an hour, the Swedish National Museum was out millions of dollars.

Over the years, the missing paintings were found. One was discovered during a narcotics investigation. Perhaps the most exciting story was the recovery of the Rembrandt self-portrait. The Swedish authorities called on the help of an FBI art recovery specialist who went deep undercover, posing as a rogue art dealer looking to purchase the Rembrandt painting. Then, in 2005, during a sting operation, the crooks were finally caught and the Rembrandt, worth thirty-six million dollars, was recovered.

A Young Parisienne

"AHHHH!" SCREAMED THE SCREAM

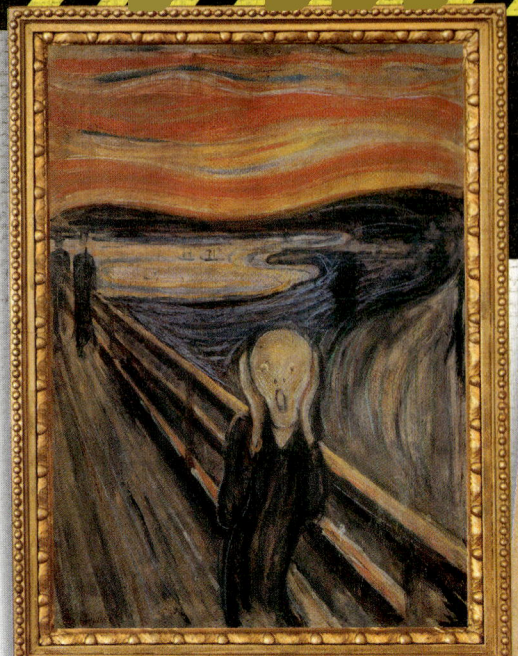

DATE: February 12, 1994
LOCATION: Oslo, Norway
MUSEUM: National Gallery
PAINTING: The Scream by Edvard Munch
THIEVES: **CAPTURED!**

Regarded as one of the best-known paintings in the world, Edvard Munch's *The Scream* has many fans, though not all of them are content with merely visiting the painting in a museum. In February 1994, two men broke into the Oslo National Gallery by climbing a ladder and smashing a window. Once inside, they used wire cutters and a small ladder to clip and snatch *The Scream* down from its hanger. Leaving the ladder and the cutters behind, the two thieves escaped with the painting in under fifty seconds. By the time the alarm went off and security was on the scene, the criminals and *The Scream* were gone.

In March, a ransom note was sent to the gallery demanding a one-million-dollar ransom for the safe return of the painting. The gallery refused to pay the ransom, however, because there was no way of knowing whether the demand was legitimate or a trick to steal more money. Then in May, police set upon several leads and found the painting unharmed in an undercover sting operation. Four men were captured and, two years later, were convicted of the crime. However, due to questionable legal issues pertaining to the sting operation, all four suspects were released.

"OH NO!" SCREAMED THE SCREAM, "NOT AGAIN!"

DATE: August 22, 2004
LOCATION: Oslo, Norway
MUSEUM: Munch Museum
PAINTING: The Scream and The Madonna by Edvard Munch
THIEVES: CAPTURED! AT LARGE!

The Scream, it would seem, is a painting so nice, it was stolen twice, but that's not completely true. You see, Edvard Munch actually created four versions of The Scream, two painted versions and two pastel versions. In 1994, one of the painted versions was stolen and found that same year in Oslo. In 2004, the second painted version was stolen, but the style of this crime was all muscle and very little brain.

In the middle of the day, two armed robbers in masks and black uniforms strolled into the Munch Museum and boldly tore two paintings by Edvard Munch down off the wall, The Scream and The Madonna. Then the thieves walked out the front door and back to their idling car. Passersby even took photographs of the event as the men walked across the lawn with the paintings in hand and stuffed them into a black Audi. Nobody was hurt and no shots were fired, but a second

Munch Museum

version of The Scream disappeared into the criminal underworld. Two years later, and after several arrests of people associated with the crime, The Scream and The Madonna were found with minimal damage. However, the two main culprits are believed to be still at large.

THE LARGEST MUSEUM HEIST IN HISTORY:
ISABELLA STEWART GARDNER MUSEUM

The Isabella Stewart Gardner Museum is located in Boston, Massachusetts, and boasts an incredible collection of historical masterpieces. However, there is one dubious claim to fame the museum wishes it didn't have... being the location of the largest museum heist in history.

The Storm on the Sea of Galilee

DATE: March 18, 1990
LOCATION: Boston, Massachusetts
MUSEUM: Isabella Stewart Gardner Museum
PAINTINGS*: The Storm on the Sea of Galilee by Rembrandt
The Concert by Johannes Vermeer
A Lady and Gentleman in Black by Rembrandt
Chez Tortoni by Édouard Manet
Landscape with an Obelisk by Govaert Flinck
Exit from Weighing by Edgar Degas
Program for an Artistic Soiree by Edgar Degas

March 17 is traditionally one of the biggest holidays of the year for Boston: St. Patrick's Day. The streets fill with revelers ready to watch the St. Patrick's Day Parade and celebrate their Irish heritage. Needless to say, St. Patrick's Day, 1990, was also one of the most hectic days of the year for the Boston city police. With so many people taking to the streets and the parade to oversee, the police force was spread thin—something the thieves of the Isabella Stewart Gardner Museum were counting on.

Late that night, two thieves disguised themselves as policemen and paid a visit to the side entrance of the museum. Over an intercom, they convinced the night guard that they were responding to a report and, breaking protocol, the night guard let the "police" inside. Instantly the men claimed that they recognized the night guard and that there was a warrant out for his arrest, which, of course, there wasn't. The night guard left his post to claim his innocence, but he also walked away from the secret alarm button, his last chance to protect the paintings in the museum.

The thieves handcuffed the guard and forced him to call the second night guard from his rounds. Once both guards were in custody, they were taken to the museum's basement and duct-taped to keep from escaping. Neither guard was harmed.

With security out of the way, the thieves roamed the halls of the museum for over eighty-one minutes, gathering thirteen priceless paintings and artifacts with cunning planning. The paintings were expertly sliced right out from their frames. There were no alarms to be triggered, so when the thieves were done, they simply left out the same side entrance where they had entered.

Program for an Artistic Soiree, Study 2 by Edgar Degas
Procession Around Florence by Edgar Degas
Self-Portrait by Rembrandt
Three Mounted Jockeys by Edgar Degas
Finial in the form of an eagle object sculpture
Chinese Bronze Beaker or Ku

THIEVES:
AT LARGE!

The estimated value of the Isabella Stewart Gardner Museum theft is five hundred million dollars, making it the largest heist ever pulled off.

Gone, but not forgotten, the empty frames still hang in the Isabella Stewart Gardner Museum to commemorate what happened and to save the space for when, or if, the masterpieces ever return.

According to Anthony Amore, the current director of security at the Gardner Museum, "The pieces that were stolen from the Gardner really are the true definition of pricelessness, because they can never be sold, they can never be replaced. So when you lose a piece from this particular collection, the museum can't just go out and acquire another masterpiece to put in its place. It has to remain empty. The spots have to remain unfilled until Mrs. Gardner's purchases and her items are put back into their proper place in the collection."

Finally, in March 2013, the FBI claimed to have a break in the infamous case. They believe that they know who stole the art. The thieves are most likely involved with the Boston Mafia. The only problem is that the twenty-year

FINIAL IN THE FORM OF AN EAGLE
One of only two objects stolen by the thieves, this was probably taken because it looked to be made of gold, when in fact it was only bronze.

LANDSCAPE WITH AN OBELISK
Long attributed to Rembrandt, this painting was finally proven to be the work of his pupil Govaert Flinck in 1980.

CHEZ TORTONI
Manet painted this work in the Parisian café Chez Tortoni, where he frequently lunched.

statute of limitations for art theft has expired, meaning the thieves can no longer be prosecuted for the art crime under federal law. So instead, the FBI is currently trying to track, locate, and recover the missing paintings. A five-million-dollar reward has been offered to anyone who can help retrieve the missing art.

THE SHORTEST-LIVED ART HEIST:
THE VAN GOGH MUSEUM

The Potato Eaters

Working fast is a hallmark of an art thief. It's usually solving the case and finding the stolen artwork that takes a long time, but not so with this 1991 robbery of the Van Gogh Museum. At closing time, two thieves hid themselves in the museum only to reemerge at 3:00 a.m. wearing ski masks and armed with guns. They quickly captured the security guards and forced them to disarm the security system, an infrared-sensing alarm that would have detected their movement in key rooms.

With the security under wraps, the thieves picked out twenty paintings and escaped at 4:47 a.m. One minute later, the guards alerted the police and the manhunt was on. All twenty paintings were found before 5:30 a.m., stashed in a Volkswagen Passat at the Amstel train station. Though the paintings were recovered, the culprits were not.

DATE: April 14, 1991
LOCATION: Amsterdam, The Netherlands
MUSEUM: The Van Gogh Museum
PAINTINGS: Sunflowers
The Potato Eaters
Still Life with Irises
Wheatfield with Crows
Still Life with Bible
THIEVES: **AT LARGE!**

22

THE VAN GOGH MUSEUM: TAKE TWO!

View of the Sea at Scheveningen

DATE: February 24, 2002
LOCATION: Amsterdam, The Netherlands
MUSEUM: The Van Gogh Museum
PAINTINGS: View of the Sea at Scheveningen
Congregation Leaving the Reformed Church in Nuenen
THIEVES: AT LARGE!

Congregation Leaving the Reformed Church in Nuenen

Eleven years after the 1991 heist, two thieves snuck into the Van Gogh Museum under cover of darkness and made off with two priceless paintings. The men used a ladder and broke through a first-story window. Though the alarm was set off, police and security forces could not get to the scene in time.

However, what the police did find was evidence: copious amounts of evidence including the ladder, the cloth the thieves used to muffle the broken window, and a cap and hat they had worn during the heist. By 2003, the police tracked down famed art thief Octave Durham, also known as "The Monkey," and his partner in crime. Octave had escaped to Spain while his partner was still living in Amsterdam. The men claimed that they were innocent, but their DNA found at the scene of the crime told a different story. Though both men served four years in prison, the paintings were never recovered.

PRICELESS PROTECTION

The challenge to museums as far as security measures is a double-edged sword. How do you keep your collection and your visitors safe while still allowing your patrons to have the full experience of engaging with the art? To truly appreciate a work of art, one really needs to be allowed to study it as closely as possible.

Luckily over the years, as technology has advanced rapidly, there are newer and smarter ways to protect museums. Updated security systems include cameras, fingerprint verifications, keypad entries, barcode cards, smart cards, contactless smart cards, and facial recognition software, all meant to better help museums track their hallowed halls at all times. That's a tall order if you consider a museum the size of the Louvre, which covers about 753,473 square feet. Here are a few ways that museums are battling the criminal element.

CAMERAS

A picture is worth a thousand words, so the more eyes you have on the paintings and on the people visiting the paintings, the better.

MOTION-DETECTING DEVICES

If a museum is empty at night, then no one will be moving around, so motion sensors are great for locating sneaky thieves. Motion sensors can also be assigned to works of art, triggering alarms if the art is touched.

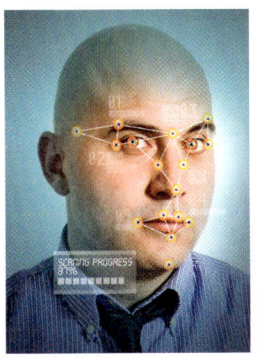

FACIAL RECOGNITION SOFTWARE

Computers are pushing the boundaries of how quickly a crime can be stopped. Facial recognition software can allow known art criminals to be traced and discovered if they ever enter another museum.

PERSONNEL

Perhaps the most important security measure to keeping a museum safe and sound is ensuring that the right people are hired in the first place to keep watch. As noted in many of the art heists described in this book, there has been a stunning amount of human error that takes place in these high-stakes situations. Plus, remember that humans are actually the brains behind all the technological security, so hiring the right security firm is also important.

WHO FINDS STOLEN ART?

Not surprisingly, most countries have no dedicated art-theft police because there are larger problems that the public faces and for police to address. But there are successful art squads within police units of certain countries where art crime is recognized as a true danger to the culture.

The FBI Art Crime Team was formed in 2004 and has successfully recovered over 2,600 items, valued at approximately $142 million. They are also responsible for maintaining the National Stolen Art File, a computerized index of reported stolen art for use by law enforcement agencies around the world.

Italy's Carabinieri Division for the Protection of Cultural Heritage stands as the oldest and largest of the world's art squads. Run by Italy's military police, the Carabinieri started in 1969. It was established after the infamous theft by Cosa Nostra of Caravaggio's *Nativity* from the Church of San Lorenzo in Palermo.

Scotland Yard in England established its Arts and Antiques Unit in 1969, but then disbanded it, only to reestablish it in 1989. Since re-forming the unit, museum theft in London has decreased by more than sixty percent, with an average annual recovery of seven million pounds (eleven million dollars) worth of stolen art.

The Netherlands Art Crime Team, known as the KLPD, was founded in 2006. They have their own national database of stolen art.

Spain and France have extensive art squads; Spain even uses YouTube to promote the recovery of stolen items.

INTERPOL is an international criminal police organization that focuses on coordinating operations between various police authorities around the world. Essentially they are a global unit working together with other countries to help fight crime. Their Stolen Works of Art Department acts as an information-gathering point for world art police, keeping track of reported crimes and stolen objects in a database and functioning as a point of reference.

Even with all of these departments searching the world for lost works, the recovery rate for stolen art remains extremely low and it is rare to find both the stolen art and successfully prosecute the criminals involved with the theft.

Founded in 1976 in an effort to bring together museums, private collectors, and authorities around the globe, the Art Loss Register is a privately owned database of lost or stolen art. It serves as a means to register and keep tabs on artwork all over the world. The register has been used as a highly successful means to search for and recover missing pieces of artwork.

In 1978, a priceless Cézanne painting, *Bouilloire et Fruits*, was stolen from a private residence in Boston. Thanks to the Art Loss Register, used extensively by the FBI and the Swiss police, the painting was able to be tracked and recovered once it came onto the black market in 1999. At the time, it was worth over twenty-nine million dollars.

In 1997, a church in Bolivia was looted of over a hundred religious artifacts. INTERPOL was brought in to investigate and the missing pieces were cataloged in the Art Loss Register. Thirteen years later, an American art dealer made inquiries about two of the stolen works, which he had purchased from another collector. Indeed they were a match—the art dealer had bought stolen artwork. The pieces, after a delicate negotiation, were returned to the Bolivian church in 2011.

The Art Loss Register currently lists 1,147 Picassos as having been reported stolen—more than the work of any other artist, which makes him the most stolen artist in the world. What makes this so amazing is that Pablo Picasso, if you remember, was himself a suspect in the theft of the *Mona Lisa* at one time. Perhaps this made his work thief-approved?

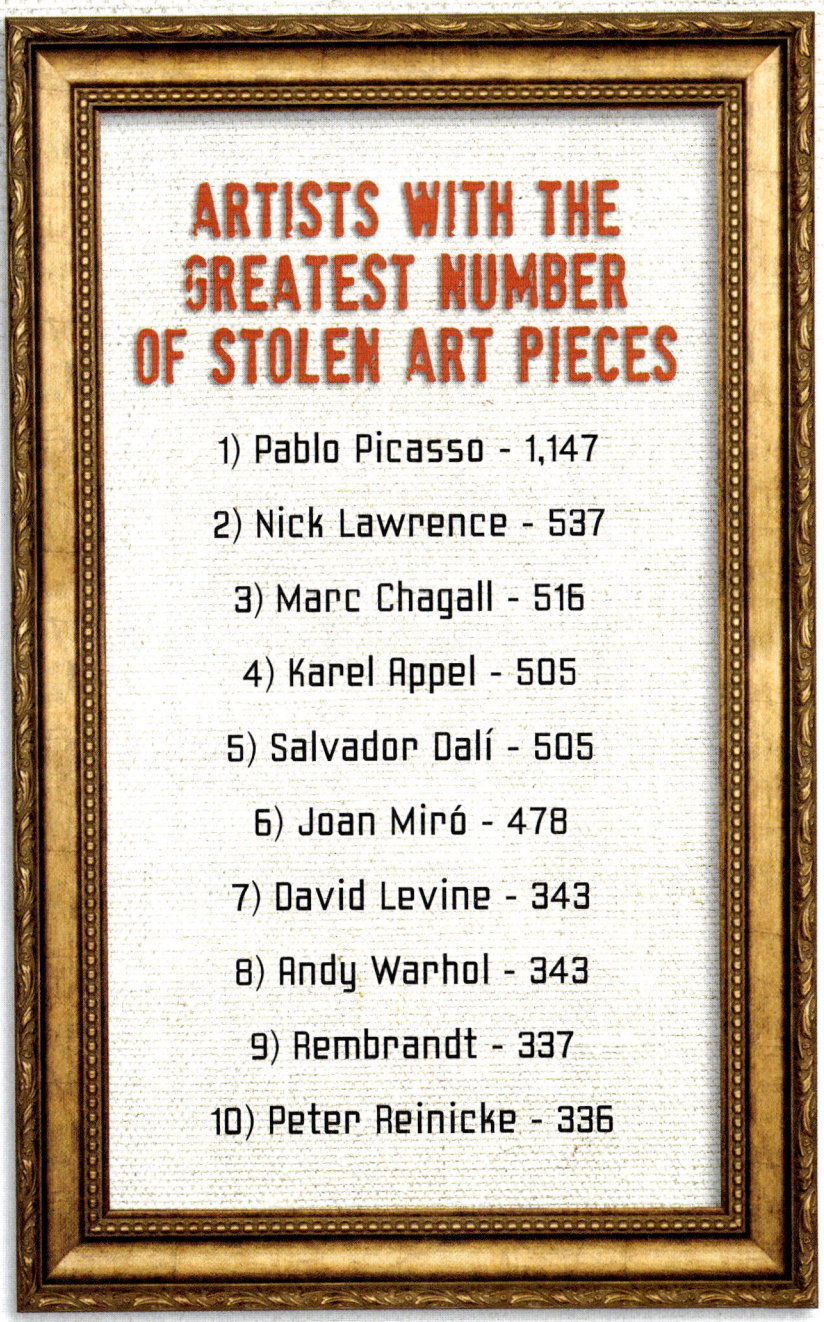

ARTISTS WITH THE GREATEST NUMBER OF STOLEN ART PIECES

1) Pablo Picasso - 1,147
2) Nick Lawrence - 537
3) Marc Chagall - 516
4) Karel Appel - 505
5) Salvador Dalí - 505
6) Joan Miró - 478
7) David Levine - 343
8) Andy Warhol - 343
9) Rembrandt - 337
10) Peter Reinicke - 336

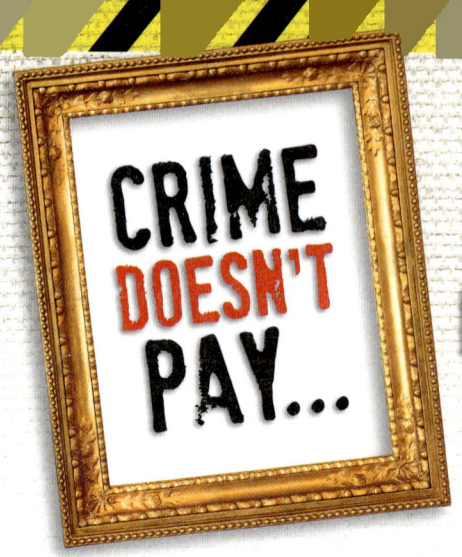

BUT ART CRIME REALLY DOESN'T PAY!

Finally, thieves who believe that they will get top dollar for stolen artwork are in for a rude awakening. The main hurdle is that a stolen masterpiece is a hot item . . . meaning that everyone in the entire world knows that it's been stolen and therefore no one in their right mind will want to buy it. To put in a bid on a stolen masterpiece is to handcuff yourself for the police on the spot. Yes, there are probably a handful of shady art dealers who exist in this murky market, but they are as rare and hard to find for the average criminal as the stolen masterpiece itself.

And even if the thieves managed to find their way into the black market, no one would ever pay full price for the stolen art. Instead, the thieves may stand to make hundreds of millions of dollars *less* for their "work." This makes the crime not worth the time. From planning the heist to risking your life, there are outrageous personal investments in art crime on the part of the criminal and most people don't fancy living their lives as fugitives from the law.

Stolen artwork can also be held for ransom, but don't count your chickens before they hatch. Most museums cannot afford to pay ransoms for stolen goods, especially since there's no guarantee that a thief is honest enough to return stolen goods and not steal the ransom money, too. So museums tend to bypass all ransom requests. Another point to consider is that the criminal who demands a ransom has now opened up a line of communication with the museum that the police will most likely use to hunt them down.

No, art crime is not a lucrative business. In fact, some would say it's about the stupidest crime business to be involved in, but art thieves have almost never proven themselves to be the smartest of sorts. Just some of the sneakiest.

Visitors to the Louvre now view the *Mona Lisa* through bulletproof glass. The famous painting was returned to the museum in 1913 after being found in Italy.

A Lady and Gentleman in Black – Rembrandt

The Concert
Johannes Vermeer

Marine
Claude Monet

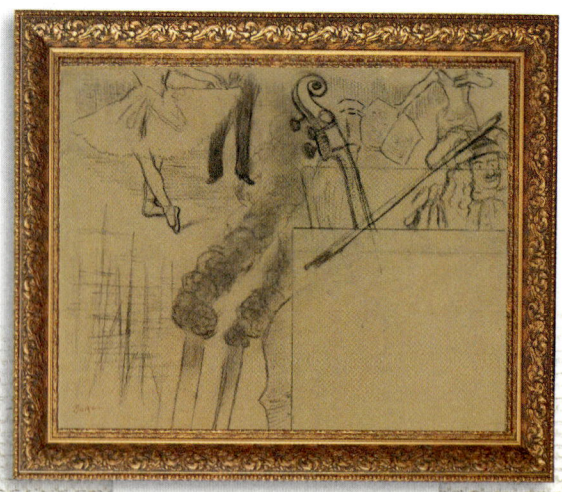

Goache drawing – Edgar Degas

32